The Blue Ball

The Blue Ball is an imaginative investigation of the experience of space, researched by the playwright among the astronauts themselves. This ambitious play questions the politics of a culture in which the wondrous is rendered mundane and what's commonplace is rendered absurd. Paul Godfrey explores the myths of the astronauts in scenes alive with irony and sharp comedy.

The Blue Ball was commissioned by the Royal National Theatre and received its première at the Cottesloe Theatre in 1995.

Paul Godfrey was born in the West Country. He trained and worked as a director in Scotland between 1982 and 1987. His work includes: *Inventing a New Colour* (Royal Court, 1988); *Once in a While the Odd Thing Happens* (Royal National Theatre, 1990); *A Bucket of Eels* (RSC Festival, 1994); *The Panic* (ROH Garden Venture, 1991); *The Blue Ball* (Royal National Theatre, 1995) and *The Modern Husband* (Actors Touring Company, 1995).

T0258362

by the same author

Once in a While the Odd Thing Happens
A Bucket of Eels & The Modern Husband

Paul Godfrey

The Blue Ball

Methuen Drama

Methuen Drama Modern Plays

First published in Great Britain 1995
by Methuen Drama

Reprinted 1995

Copyright © 1995 by Paul Godfrey
The author has asserted his moral rights

ISBN 0–413–68820–8

A CIP catalogue record for this book
is available from the British Library

Front cover: view of the Earth from Apollo 17, courtesy of
NASA

Typeset by Wilmaset, Birkenhead, Wirral

Caution

All rights whatsoever in this play are strictly reserved and
application for performance etc., should be made before
rehearsals begin to A. P. Watt, 20 John Street, London
WC1N 2DR. No performance may be given unless a licence
has been obtained.

Lost In Space?

Like the actor Gina in this play, I have touched the moon, touched it with the hand that writes these words. What moved me wasn't that the rock came from the moon but that millions of fingers had imparted a metallic sheen to its surface, reflecting a meaning and importance delivered by the attention of all those people.

On the shelf in my room I have a small plate by William Blake of a ladder to the moon and someone climbing up, its caption reads: I WANT! I WANT!

Thanks to NASA the fast fulfilment of this precise aspiration is now open to everyone at the Air and Space Museum in Washington, where they keep the only piece of the moon on earth that's available for the public touch.

*   *   *

Few would seriously consider their lives ruled by the planets, yet the universe has us in its grip as surely as if we were chess pieces. I sit and write my play. The calendar describes an outline of months while my clock counts the hours of each day. I may choose how to spend time but the structure itself is predetermined by our place in the solar system. A year is the time it takes to orbit the sun, a month is a cycle of the moon and in a day the earth revolves once. Alter any of these factors and it would all be entirely different. If we were in another relationship to the sun then our years would be longer or shorter and consequently it would have taken me a different number of years to write this play.

The first human stepped onto the moon when I was eight. In my childhood it had no larger significance than anything that occurred beyond the immediate domestic world. This was something that happened one school lunch time. I never quite connected the event with the moon in the sky and when our television broke shortly after I was spared the repetitions of the subsequent Apollo missions. A century earlier Jules Verne wrote of men travelling to the moon from Florida, so even before it happened the event had been overtaken by fiction. My father knew a man in his eighties who didn't believe they had actually been there, to him it wasn't possible, he denied it as a hoax. Born six months before Yuri Gagarin became the first human in space in 1961, I was an unwitting child of this space age.

It was an eclipse that brought me to recognise where I was. In those rare seconds as the planets converged and parted again I had before my eyes the evidence of my position as a traveller in a moving universe. I was standing still on the back lawn but this familiar patch of green turf was being hurled across the universe at an inconceivable rate. We live in space, and when I see the sun drop below the horizon or the moon rise into the sky I remember this.

The poetry of TV weather forecasts is astounding: see the map with images of the sun scattered across it and sometimes stars too! There appears to be no contradiction in reconciling this medieval fantasy with satellite photographs, which confirms my belief that in our hearts we live in a pre-Copernican universe which has the earth as its centre and the sun in orbit around us. This perspective is reflected in our language, not just *sunrise* and *sunset* but expressions like 'when the sun comes out' or 'the waxing and waning of the moon'. As if they weren't there all the time.

Who does not sympathise with Pablo Picasso who on the day of the moon landing said 'It means nothing to me, I have no opinion and I don't care'? Eugene Ionesco acknowledged this indifference writing on the same day, 'The sign that it's so important is that most people aren't interested in it. They go on discussing sentimental affairs.'

In 1990 when I set out on my quest to find this play I had no idea how long it would take or where it would lead. It fascinates me that an experience as fundamentally wondrous as our first forays into space could have been rendered mundane in such a short time and I wanted to explore how this paradox could be.

Imagine my discomfort when I met my first astronaut and as they walked into the room I discovered in that instant that I didn't believe it, knew it, yes, but believed it barely. My doubts surfaced as I explored the Lyndon Johnson Space Center in Houston where astronauts are trained. As I walked the hundred yards' length of the Saturn V rocket laid out on the grass, its primitivism appalled me, like an early steam engine in a museum, all the welds were visible and the words painted on by a signwriter. Its first fifteen feet comprised the capsule for the people and the rest was simply a canister of fuel, stood on end and lit. Passing from the rocket I came across one of the capsules, expecting the sleekness of mass-produced technology; instead I found scuffed pieces of metal riveted together and interlaced with a tangle of wires. The space suits were hand-stitched in places. Running my hand along the outside of the tiny capsule burnt to the colour of ashes, pitted and scored by the furnace temperature of the earth's atmosphere, I could scarcely comprehend how this do-it-yourself enterprise had worked.

Next I went to see the moon rocks in their storage building, constructed to withstand all natural disasters and nuclear explosions too. The enigmatic stones are kept in pure nitrogen, to prevent rusting, within transparent boxes. From behind bullet proof glass in the viewing facility I scrutinised these intractable pieces of granite. They were cherished like babies in incubators except these weren't alive, they were dead rocks.

Once I overcame my disbelief I was assaulted by the irony in the choice of the most rational individuals in order to propel them into the mysterious. At first it was frustratingly difficult to get any sense at all from the astronauts of what it was like. I was beginning to realise that there probably weren't answers to some of my questions, and I recognised a powerful desire to experience some of this wonder for myself.

I arrived in Cape Canaveral during the spring break. One road runs parallel to the ocean and the motels that fill the space between were riddled with spring breakers: students partying, drinking and frantically coupling. Four days until the launch of the space shuttle Atlantis. The surfing stores had shelves of launch souvenirs, tariff boards carried good luck messages to the crew and each hotel reception had its display of signed astronaut photographs. It was a relief to escape an English April and be in the Florida sunshine. I got an astronaut haircut.

The launch was scheduled for 8 a.m. At 5 a.m. when I climbed into my taxi it was raining. The freeway was already busy and the driver explained it would reach a standstill within an hour. Several hundred thousand people drive overnight across country to see each launch.

At the gates to the space centre I was assigned a security guard who escorted me to the press compound. We drove along a causeway through a swamp, oranges hung in the dark undergrowth of dawn and ditches on either side had notices: BEWARE THIS DRAINAGE DITCH IS INFESTED WITH POISONOUS SNAKES. My driver told me the story of the jealous astronaut who killed a six-foot snake, placed it under the desk of a colleague moon-bound with the next Apollo mission, and then telephoned to summon him to his desk, for a joke.

The press room is an eighty-foot dome with desks in concentric circles. I staked out a space between 'Newsweek' and 'Scientific American' boldly chalking the words 'Royal National Theatre' on the desk label. Thousands of pigeon-holes line the outer wall of the building, in each one a different press release. Most of the newsmen were watching the astronauts suiting up on close circuit TV. Once I'd acquired a pile of literature I went outside in search of action.

Overshadowing everything stands the VAB (Vehicle Assembly Building)*, the biggest building in the world, they claim. In here it's possible to construct a Saturn V rocket and wheel it out on end. Beneath this grey monolith sits Mission Control. To my right was a primitive stadium built of steel girders, behind it the tent for sponsors (DEDICATED TO DISCOVERING THE ORIGINS OF SPACE AND TIME) and on my left were the TV vans. Straight ahead was the digital clock, each side of a digit the length of a fluorescent tube, and behind it half a mile away across the lake was the space shuttle. TV crews were preparing their stake-outs, with shuttle in left distance, immaculate news readers stood on wet grass practising their reports.

I walked past the great big clock down to the lakeside to see if the alligators were stirring yet. Rain flecked the sky. Pelicans circled over me but the lake dwellers did not show,

---

*Parentheses, to give them their Latin name *lunulae*, are derived from ancient pictograms of the phases of the moon used to denote a passage of time.

like the shuttle they were waiting for the sun. I could only speculate at the emotions of those who gathered here to watch Apollo 11 launch the first men to the moon in 1969 or the space shuttle Challenger that took its crew of seven to their deaths in 1986 when a booster rocket exploded.

After several hours in the stadium reading NASA press releases I began to get excited by the countdown. With less than an hour to go the rhythm of the digital clock seemed to penetrate the air. The rain stopped. At ten minutes the launch was held for five to allow the clouds to clear. High-flying jets reported a launch window approaching.

When the countdown resumed everyone came out onto the lawn. The launch was going ahead. It was a curious social event, the crowd standing silent looking to the horizon. A minute to go. The launch pad was as still as it ever was. Then, as if planned, there was a gap in the clouds exactly overhead. Ten seconds to go and a charge travelled through the crowd. We all counted in unison. At two seconds, clouds of smoke swelled from under the shuttle. Zero, and nothing happened. It doesn't fly right up into the air like a rocket should!

Nothing happened and I held my breath. The tiny white shuttle in the distance vibrated with a violence I cannot describe. It didn't ascend though. I was thinking why is there no sound? Why doesn't it move? I watched it rise for a couple of seconds just clear of the horizon, still vibrating and then the shock hit me. Palm trees struck the ground; I learnt why the stadium is made only of girders and the alligators got their morning call. Journalists and photographers were stumbling and staggering. Still the shuttle was barely above the horizon.

The shuttle rose in a gentle spiral trailing a delicate plume of smoke. A cloud bank took it from us at the moment the booster rockets were jettisoned and when it reappeared we were simply watching a bright light up in the sky. Then it was gone, as if through a ceiling. We are used to seeing aeroplanes fly away and diminish but this vanishing seemed to surprise everyone. People exchanged comments and several rubbed their necks and then they all began to drift in the direction of breakfast in the NASA canteen. As the crowd moved faces turned back at the sky. I looked as well, just to check it had really gone. In the press room a TV monitor was showing the launch view from the inside of the shuttle:

Cape Canaveral receding, then azure sky blending to cerulean and then the darkness of space.

When I returned in less than an hour a winking light on an illuminated map of the world revealed that the shuttle had orbited the earth in less than the time it took to eat my breakfast (I eat quickly). Already it was off across the Atlantic for the second time that morning.

The day was the thirtieth anniversary of the flight of Yuri Gagarin. President Kennedy's encouragement of the Apollo programme was a response to the Russian space initiative. Bluntly, both competitors in the space race wanted to prove they had the best rockets and could nuke the other first if necessary. It wasn't peace that took men to the moon, this race was a central but incidental contest in the Cold War.

How was I to know if all I had learnt wasn't simply the American experience? Four days later I sat in a hotel room and choked with relief to watch the shuttle land safely. If I wanted to isolate the experience itself I needed to learn what was common among astronauts and cosmonauts in both countries. I switched the television off and decided to go to Russia and hear the other story.

By chance I picked the month that the Soviet Union collapsed, December 1991. Dina and Arkady, two editors of *Theatre* magazine were my hosts. They arranged a place for me to stay in a block on the outskirts of Moscow and introduced me to interpreters.

In Moscow, at the Exhibition of Economic Achievements in the Space Dome I had the privilege to attend the first rave to be held in the former USSR. THE YURI GAGARIN PARTY, held on his birthday, which was perhaps more of an excuse than a celebration of him. The Space Dome is where they display the spacecraft and Gagarin's capsule was suspended above the crowd, just visible through the smoke, lasers and moving projections of his smiling face. Arkady and I stood among the heaving masses. He had visited the exhibition once before as a child and young communist pioneer. Overcome with the emotion of the moment he exclaimed 'This is the end of the Soviet Union!' He was right. The exhibition space is now a used-car lot.

At Star City on the outskirts of Moscow where they train cosmonauts, I visited the replica of Gagarin's office. Here is his diary open at the day his plane crashed. Today the cosmonauts come and sign their names in it before each flight. There's been no adequate explanation of his early death. I even heard a rumour that he was still alive somewhere in a remote Soviet mental institution. Perhaps the authorities killed him, wary of his international reputation and fearing he could speak out? Perhaps it was simply an accident? Or perhaps it was suicide? I asked myself why the first man in space should wish to kill himself.

Gagarin's body is in the Kremlin Wall on Red Square. He's almost the only figure from the communist era for whom young Russians have any respect. If it's possible to imagine a time when the names of Lenin and Stalin are forgotten then in that time surely people will come here to the place where Yuri Gagarin lies.

Westerners had only been admitted to Star City a few months previously. There were still people who had worked here in the early days. They told me that before Gagarin's flight almost no one but the chief engineer and Gagarin himself believed it could work. I was excited to meet cosmonauts, though they were more excited to meet me when they heard I had bottles of vodka. I tried to set up a visit to a launch in Baikonur from where they propelled Gagarin into space but circumstances conspired against me. Only later did I discover that Kazakhstan where the launch facility is situated was declaring itself independent of the Soviet Union at that moment.

At the Russian Academy of Science, where for unknown reasons they presented me with a medal, I had the pleasure to spend some time with Svetlana Savitskaya, the second women in space and the first to do a space walk. Shortly after Gagarin the Russians put a woman in space to prove it could be done. This woman, Valentina Tereshkova had been selected for her politically appropriate background and had a mirror attached to her space suit to check her make-up in space. When high temperature and air pressure caused her to pass out in orbit she was accused of falling asleep and no other woman got to be a cosmonaut for many years until Svetlana overcame the resistance.

She was fourteen when she saw Valentina's flight and decided then to do it herself. She practised gymnastics at

school until she made the Olympic team. In further education
she studied astronomy and engineering, she joined the college
flying corps and achieved a pilot's licence to aerobatic
standard. Next she applied to join the space programme and
though they were not taking women they were forced to accept
her as she was more qualified than any man. But they didn't
forgive her for her fiercely independent womanhood.

Now this was the first time men and women had been
together in space so when they returned to earth the
technicians asked the men 'Did you fuck her?' 'Svetlana!'
they replied, 'You must be joking!' I don't wish to imply that
this misogyny is unique to the Russians because it was not
until much later, in the early eighties, that the Americans
chose to put a woman in space. Twelve middle-aged white
men were sent to the moon.

On my last day the mission controller at Star City asked
me if it would help me with my play to speak to the men
orbiting on the space station Mir. These cosmonauts had
recently been informed that the Soviet Union was over, that
it was uncertain when they could return to earth and now
they were asked to speak to a playwright from the Royal
National Theatre in London.

My research has never been academic, I'm seeking to
extend my imaginative world. As I spoke to these cosmonauts
they completed half an orbit of the earth, I no longer doubted
the reality of it and I recognised the full impact of the wonder
of the experience, as much as I ever shall.

If I hadn't done all the research I couldn't have written this
play, or rather, not *this* play. In total, perhaps I spoke to
twenty-five astronauts and cosmonauts; they were as different
as twenty-five people could be and these differences could not
be said to fall into any pattern that matches the cultural
divisions of east and west. I learnt that for people living and
working in a space programme there is a common experience
that exists irrespective of national identity, and I found it was
possible using my own language, to create scenes and
characters in a space programme that explored this experience
itself. These scenes are informed equally by my first-hand
knowledge of both the Russian and American space programmes
and I make this explicit in the final dialogue when the audience
learns that the playwright is going to visit the cosmonauts.

If you ask an American who was the first in space they will say either Alan Shepard (the first above the earth's atmosphere) or John Glenn (the first to orbit the earth), they will be unlikely to say Yuri Gagarin (the first of all). The first human in space is already a figure of mythology. I have called him Alex.

In the play I chose to set all the research scenes I created in America. This decision was taken for several reasons: I couldn't have scenes in Russia without including the fall of communism, and that's another story. The play is written for an English-speaking audience, we have constructed our view from the American experience and I wanted to show how this had come about. Finally, I was reluctant to create a convention for characters who spoke Russian and further complicate a complex play. Ironically I know the time in Russia brought me to see the Americans more clearly, enabling me to portray their society in the research scenes. So I am aware that the experience in Russia is present in every aspect of this play.

It took me eighteen months to undertake these trips, this includes the time I spent raising the money, negotiating ways into the programmes, as well as making the visits. It was to be another eighteen months' work to complete the script. I'd already written some material but now I had to find a way to use playwriting to confront this experience.

Only eight months later did the club sandwich structure of the play arrive. I searched for a means to bring the experience into the here and now for an audience in the theatre. This subject, by its nature, engenders disbelief and I needed to bring an audience to recognise their relationship to it, and accept it as an immediate reality. I chose to place a character in the play who came from the world the audience knows, the playwright. If they can accept the truth of the research scenes then I hope the structure of the play may lead an audience to believe the whole thing.

I've come to recognise there's a chasm between knowledge and belief. Theatre draws upon the capacity we have to accept as real what we know to be enacted, and within this acceptance to embrace simultaneous dramatic worlds. I have put together the two sides of my play like a pair of opposing mirrors so that within an infinite range of perspectives each member of the audience may place themselves in relation to what they see, according to what they believe.

The experience of writing is such an entirely absorbing process that I have almost no memory of this time while I was writing the play. As the months passed money got scarcer and I moved out of a room by the river to rent a cheaper one in a council block by the Barbican. From the eighth floor I could look down on Bunhill Fields where William Blake is buried. Finally I couldn't afford this room any more and I moved into a tiny office with one tap and no phone, at the edge of the city. I covered the walls with pictures of the earth from space. Here I worked and here I lived and eventually finished the play.

For a brief spell I was proud to tell people they'd never meet anyone who knew as many astronauts as I did. It redefines *starfucker* doesn't it? From several quarters I discovered the urban myth of the mad astronauts: 'They're all crazy now aren't they?' I quickly learnt to keep my mouth shut or I'd be groping for words in response to the question that has no simple answer: 'What are they like?'

Perhaps the reader may wonder what the relationship is between me and the character of the playwright? Let me put it clearly, he is the one in the play who's going to write the play in the play whereas I am the one who wrote the play.

This introduction, written as the play went into production for publication at its opening, exists without the benefit of hindsight that will be available to the reader. In my experience the most interesting plays are not always about what they're *about*, content and subject rarely coincide. So I must leave you here to your own conclusion.

This work could not have existed without the faith that Richard Eyre and Giles Croft showed in the idea from its conception in 1990. Over these years their support has encouraged me on what's been a long and eventful journey.

Paul Godfrey
Royal National Theatre
1995

for my father
the aircraft engineer

'. . . the fortune of us that are the Moones men doeth ebbe and flow like the Sea, beeing governed as the Sea is, by the Moone.'

Henry IV, I

'I didn't go into space just to return and open supermarkets.'

Helen Sharman

This play was begun in the summer of 1990 and completed in the summer of 1993.

Let me acknowledge all the astronauts who spoke to me of their experiences; the Association of Space Explorers who put me in touch; and the David Harlech Memorial Bursary (1990) and the Stephen Arlen Award (1991) which enabled me to undertake the visits.

Grants from the Polonsky Foundation, the Arts Council and the Society of Authors funded me to finish the script.

Although I have included scenes of research, the play is entirely a work of fiction.

Characters

Alex, *the best pilot (20s)*
Dan, *a pilot (20s)*
Stone, *the top scientist (50s)*
Carl, *a pilot (20s)*
Sylvie, *an astronaut (30s)*
Paul, *the playwright (30s)*
Anna, *Alex's wife (20s)*
Roger, *an astronomer (30s)*
Judy, *a doctor (30s)*
Bob, *an astronaut (40s)*
Nell, *Bob's wife (40s)*
Oliver, *an astronaut (60s)*
Gina, *an actor (40s)*
Several pilots

The research scenes take place in America in the present day while the other parts of the play refer to a time thirty years before. I wish the audience to understand that the scenes with Alex take place within a space programme that's neither American nor Russian but something created by the playwright: a synthesis of the two.

The Blue Ball received its première at the Cottesloe Theatre, Royal National Theatre, London, on 23 March 1995 with the following cast:

Alex	Dexter Fletcher
Dan	Mason Phillips
Stone	Nigel Terry
Carl	Nicolas Tennant
Sylvie	Annabelle Apsion
Paul	Peter Darling
Anna	Pooky Quesnel
Roger	George Anton
Judy	Sonia Ritter
Bob	William Armstrong
Nell	Gabrielle Lloyd
Oliver	Trevor Peacock
Gina	Annabelle Apsion

Directed by Paul Godfrey
Designed by Stewart Laing
Music by David Sawer
Lighting by Mimi Jordan Sherin

Several pilots including **Alex**, **Dan** *and* **Carl**.

Several pilots
Now we are going to find out the truth.
Which of us is it to be?
The man knows.
I know.
We all know, everyone knows.
Each of us thinks it's him.

Alex
I don't know, I have no idea.

Dan
It could be any one of us.

Stone *enters*.

Stone
Here's the decision. (*Picks* **Alex**.) It's you.
(*Picks* **Dan**.) And you will be the standby.
(*To* **Alex**.) What's your reaction?

Alex
I'm pleased . . . I'm grateful.

Stone
You must never be grateful
because we're not being generous here.

Alex
It's all I hoped.
Everyone looks to the sky.

Stone
You've no fear?

Alex
I know there's the possibility of that emotion
but I've learnt to overcome it
(unleashing a blind panic can risk the success of a flight
and endanger the lives of others).

Stone
Aren't you frightened of death?

Alex
When I became an airman I found I could accept death.
It surprised me.

Stone
You have children don't you?

Alex
Yes, to be here when I'm gone.

Stone
You don't value your existence very highly?

Alex
Whether I live or die you offer the chance of something else.

Stone
So you are prepared to stake your life?

Alex
I am happy to do this.
You need the best pilot.
I understand that.

Stone
All I need at this moment
is for you to believe this.

Alex
I believe it.

Stone (*to the others*)
When he succeeds you will all be next.
Everything will be possible
once we have done this.
For the next thirty-six hours
you two will prepare,
both of you will go out onto the launch site
and only then
will one step forward.
Now you all have one last duty together
before we part here
and that is to record this moment.

They line up for a photograph.

Dan (*aside*)
Even if it was a sentence of death
he seemed happy and unware.
For thirty-six hours
as his shadow
I began to believe
I was him.
I saw no difference between us.
We both had the same training.
I couldn't figure it out.
Why was it him and not me?
I was angry with envy.
When it came to the moment
I nearly stepped forward
that's how close I came to it.
I was surprised to find myself walking away.
Later when they fired the rocket
there was an inferno of flames
and I was sick with relief.
On the radio he was laughing.
I was glad to be safe.
Thank God they didn't pick me.

Carl (*to* **Alex**)
We wish you well.
We count this no dishonour
because we are all your friends here.
We were proud to know you.

Alex
Thank you.
I'll take your names with me.
You must all sign a piece of paper
and I'll put it in my pocket.
Now, let's begin. I know what to do.

Exit **Stone**, **Alex** *and* **Dan**.

Carl
Who wants to make a bet?
No?
I don't believe it can work either.
Now we are going to find out the truth.

2

Sylvie *and* **Paul**.

Sylvie
I admit it, I am ordinary.

Paul
You're the first astronaut I've met.

Sylvie
There's nothing special about me.

Paul
What is it like in space?

Sylvie
Being in space, I'd say it was
more incredible than you could imagine . . .

Paul
So what surprised you?

Sylvie
Everything.
Nothing could prepare you for that.

Paul
Can you be more specific?

Sylvie
Yes, the *whole* experience was a surprise.

Paul
In this play what must I show?

Sylvie
You've got to tell them about the wonder of it,
how overwhelming that is.

Paul
Do you talk about it much,
have you given many interviews?

Sylvie
Are you kidding?
We're trained to talk in soundbites here.

Paul
I am not a journalist
you can tell me whatever you want.
Why not talk about your emotions?
You said it was overwhelming.

Sylvie
Yes, but there's no room for emotion in space.

Paul
Isn't wonder an emotion?

Sylvie
Emotions are irrelevant to an astronaut.
If you were to think about it you could feel helpless.

Paul
You learn to deny emotion?

Sylvie
It has its place, afterwards.
You should see our touchdown parties.

Paul
I'm glad I met you first.

Sylvie
Why?

Paul
Because you're a woman.

Sylvie
So?

Paul
Do women have a different view of space?

Sylvie
Gender and race aren't issues here.
I don't see myself as a woman.
Being an astronaut is more significant
than any racial or gender difference.

Paul
It's simply that I know most astronauts are white and male.

Sylvie
NASA tries to be an equal opportunities employer.

Paul
Except when it comes to moon landings?

Sylvie
Look, if you know what it is you want to learn,
then ask me and I'll tell you.

Paul
I don't have an answer to that.
Whatever I find I can use
but writing a play is primarily an act of the imagination.

Sylvie
Is that so?
I'm not ashamed to admit that I have no imagination at all.

Paul
I don't believe you.

Sylvie
We work to fulfil the expectations placed upon us.
Imagination is not one of them.
We're trained to analyse a situation then act,
to think and then speak,
but I admit this is a new situation for me
talking to a playwright.

Paul
How can I grasp this experience you've had?
It's a wonder to me.
Talking about it here now, it seems unreal.

Sylvie
Why should anything be more wondrous
than anything else?
Why should it be more wondrous for me to go up in orbit
than to be here having a conversation with you?

Paul
Here we are in a room,
there you were out in space.

Sylvie
Here we are.
There's a sense in which we are in space now.

Paul
Travelling through space now.

Sylvie
Exactly, it's a wonder we can stand up at all isn't it?

Paul
That's true, but it's commonplace;
your experience is new entirely.
That's what I want to know about.

Sylvie
Look, I'm doing my best
I'm telling you about me,
what I'm like;
and what it's like in space.
Aren't you getting a picture now?

Paul
Let me try a different question.
Do you like it in space?

Sylvie
Me, I would go even if I could never come back.

Paul
I've never met anyone like you.
Are you famous?
Do people recognise you in the street?

Sylvie
Now and again people recognise me here,
there are so many astronauts around
but elsewhere no one would pick me from a crowd,
there's nothing extraordinary about me.

Paul
Isn't there?

Sylvie
WHAT?

3

Anna
We rise in the dark
and he leaves me in the dawn.
Each morning I am full of hope
even if the routine is mundane.

I didn't have many choices,
I knew marriage was inevitable,
I left home and went to a typing school.
That was my bid for freedom.

We met the pilots at the base.
They knew we were easy
but I wasn't that interested
so I became a prize
then I was able to choose between them.

I got the best pilot,
and everyone hated me for it.

Alex *enters*.

Alex
It's me they've picked.

Anna
I knew it.
I needed this.

Alex
We worked hard.

Anna
I dreamed of flight.

Alex
Now we've got something,
it's been worth it.

Anna
We made every sacrifice.
I never had anything.

Alex
Are you pleased?

Anna
Everyone will treat us differently now.

Alex
Need they?

Anna
They had better.

Alex
I met the top scientist.
I knew I could trust him instantly.

Anna
I'm so happy.

Alex
We can't tell anyone.

Anna
I don't mind not telling anyone
because we'll be rich.

Alex
Don't be petty.
I'll get no more money.

Anna
Not yet.
But the day will come.

Alex
Will it?

Anna
What shall I tell the children?

Alex
Tell them their father is an extraordinary man.

Anna
I knew you were unique.

Alex
I'm unique now.

Anna
When is it?

Alex
Tomorrow, after midnight,
less than thirty-six hours.

Anna
What shall I do?
How can I be ready?

Alex
Now I've told you,
now I have to go.

Anna
What if you don't come back?

Alex
I don't know.

Anna
What's going to happen?

Alex
I don't know.

Anna
I'm never going to see you again.

Alex
No.

Anna
Kiss me.

Alex
Don't squeeze the life out of me!

Anna
You've plenty of life in you.

Alex
Goodbye.

Anna
What's to become of me?
Don't go.

Alex
Don't be frightened.

Anna
I'm not frightened, I'm greedy for you.

Alex
I'm not frightened either.

Anna
You're mad then.

Alex
I'm lost?

Anna
Not yet.
Go.
Go and come back.

Alex
I'll go and come back just the same as I am now.

Exits.

Anna
If they kill him could I manage to start again?

4

Paul, **Roger** *and* **Judy**.

Paul
Here are the phone numbers of all the Apollo astronauts:
who shall I call first?
Shall I call Neil?

Roger
Neil? Don't bother.

Paul
Shouldn't I talk to Neil?

Roger
No, I should forget him.
Cross him off the list.

Judy
Why do you want to meet astronauts,
they're merely human like everyone else aren't they?

Roger
Neil Armstrong gave a lecture at the astronomy faculty.
He spoke for two hours about the moon
and never mentioned that he'd been there.

Paul
I had the chance to travel, a small grant,
and I thought who in the world would I most like to meet.

Judy
Now you've met one; what was he like?

Paul
She, she was extraordinary.
She said she had no imagination.

Roger
Did you ask what it was like in space?

Paul
She said it was more incredible than you could imagine.

Roger
Wow.

Judy
It can't be difficult for something to be more incredible than
you can imagine when you have no imagination.

Paul *dials*.

Paul
This is Alan Bean, the astronaut who's taken to painting,
perhaps he'll understand what I'm about?

Judy
Why should an astronaut be more interesting than anyone
else?

Paul
I want to know about the experience of being in space.

Roger
You need to learn some astronomy.

Paul
OK, explain what it is you do exactly.

Roger
I work in the search for the missing matter.
You know that most of the mass of the Universe is missing?

Paul
He's not there. No?

Roger
We can see what there is where there's light
so . . .

Call answers.

Paul
(Hello. This is Paul Godfrey.
Did you get my letter?)

Roger
. . . I look where there's darkness
where there doesn't seem to be anything.

Paul
(I'm here researching a play
and I'd like to come and talk to you.)

Judy
There are plenty of actual wonders he should take in.

Paul
What's an actual wonder?

Judy
The Grand Canyon
or the Niagara Falls
or even the Great Plains.

Roger
That 97 per cent of the Universe is missing.

Paul
(Can I come and talk to you while you're painting?)

Roger
We know it exists but no one can find it.

Judy
You go there and you still can't believe it.

Paul
(I am interested in how astronauts behave before and after they've been in space.)

Judy
Something like that you can't hold it all in your head.

Paul
(I want to see how your paintings communicate what it's like in space.)

Roger
I believe that what we can't see must be somewhere we can't see it.

Paul
(No, there's no budget to pay you a fee.)

Roger
So I am hoping I might just find something.

Judy
You mean 'nothing'?

Paul
(I've nothing like that kind of money.)

Judy
It wouldn't be *anything* would it?

Paul
(Let me buy you lunch.)

Judy
Not if you look where there's nothing.

Paul
(Don't you take a break?
Why not have lunch?)

Roger
But if I found it it would be something.

Paul
(But if you can eat while you're painting,
why can't you talk while you're painting?)

Judy
If you can find something where there's nothing
then that would be an actual wonder.

Paul
He cut me off.

Roger
Are you disappointed?

Paul
Well no, I talked to a man who walked on the moon.

Judy
Did he say anything good?

Paul
You heard the conversation.
It was either buy a painting or pay a fee.

Judy
I work with a woman who's married to an astronaut,
I'm sure you can meet him
while you are staying with us.

Roger
I'd be interested to meet an astronaut too.

Paul
Could I talk to both of them?

Roger
Let's all do dinner.

Judy
OK, I'll call her.

5

Anna *and* **Stone**.

Anna
Is he here now?

Stone
Yes. In a moment he'll come

and you can have a few minutes alone.
Now we need to talk first.
It's this: if he has any after-effects you must tell me.

Anna
Will he be changed?
Is something wrong?

Stone
No. I believe he will be unchanged
but I don't want him to hold anything to himself.

Anna
He's honest.
He's an honest man.

Stone
If there are any ill-effects, I must know.
You must tell me;
but we don't want him to feel uncomfortable
so I don't want him to know this.

Anna
I understand.

Stone
It's in his interest.
It's in all our interests.

Anna
All that matters to me
is that he's still alive.

Stone
He's alive. Are we agreed?

Anna
Yes.

Alex *enters with blood on his face.*

Alex
I am the luckiest man alive.

Stone
My children . . .

Stone *exits.*

Anna
Is this your hand?

Alex
Yes, I hope so.

Anna
Is this your body?

Alex
Yes, I think so.

Anna
It's you, I'm sure.

Alex
An orbit of the entire earth
in a hundred minutes of my life.

Anna
What was it like?

He looks at her.

And you're safe?
You're shaking.

Alex
I'm here.
I can just stand
but I can feel the gravity pulling me down.

Anna
God.
Did you see God?

Alex
No, but I looked.

Anna
If you didn't see Him then where is He?

Alex
It was a small window, I had a camera, but no telescope.

Anna
Did you see the stars?

Alex
Yes. And the moon too.
The sun rose twice.

Anna
I thought you would die.

Alex
It all worked well enough.

Anna
Our children are asleep.
Everything is as it was.

Alex
Everything happens once doesn't it?
Only once for the first time:
this is that moment.

Anna
It's not in everyone's destiny to get a glimpse of heaven.

Alex
I saw the world turning.

Anna
Does it revolve like a school globe?

Alex
Yes.

Anna
Who could believe that?

Alex
I believe my eyes.

Anna
Tell me about the stars.

Alex
They don't sparkle.

Anna
How is that?

Alex
It's the sky that diffuses the light.

Anna
It's not real then?

Alex
Does it matter?

Anna
I need to believe my eyes too.
Tell me is the earth green?

Alex
It's blue.

Anna
Like the sky?

Alex
Like the sea.

Anna
How? Water has no colour.

Alex
The sky itself is transparent from above,
I saw the blue sky reflected into the blue sea.
From space even the sun is a bluish colour,
not yellow at all.

Anna
In an hour the sun will rise.

Alex
No.

Anna
The sun always rises.

Alex
The sun never rises.

Anna
What then?

Alex
The earth is revolving.

Anna
You said the sun *rose* twice.

Alex
I did, didn't I?
That shows how quickly you can forget.

Dan *enters.*

Alex
I'm telling her what I saw.
All these things competing with each other.
How can I separate the thoughts from the sensations
and the sensations from the sights
and the sights from the thoughts?
How will there ever be the words
to disentangle them all?

Anna
My heart is beating like a drum.
I tell you, I shall look at the sky differently now.

Alex (*to* **Dan**)
Here's the paper, here are your names
that I took with me.

Dan
The same piece of paper.
We won't divide it, we'll keep it whole.

Alex
Nothing in my life can ever match this.

Stone *enters.*

Anna (*to* **Stone**)
He looks no worse than he did sometimes
after what he suffered in training.

Stone
I rely on you to create a normal existence for him.

Alex
I'll be myself again soon.

Stone
I'd like you to have more children
prove to the world you are still a man.

Alex
Back for the rest of my life.

Dan
And now it begins.

6

Judy, **Bob**, **Nell**, **Paul**, **Roger** *in a restaurant.*

Judy (*aside*)
Perhaps I am the only person in this town
who doesn't want to go into space?
It holds no interest for me.

Perhaps you wonder how I get on with him
when his universe is at the end of a telescope
and mine is here and now?

Perhaps you noticed
I am not a tolerant person?
It isn't in my nature.
Tolerance is not admitting you disagree;
I disagree, that's my nature.

Tolerance is a meagre virtue,
I prefer generosity
because that's bigger.

All of which means
simply by arranging dinner
for this playwright to meet an astronaut
I am able to feel good about my intolerance.

Bob (*to* **Paul**)
You must understand that though I am an astronaut
I still am an essentially ordinary man;
it's simply that I have been lucky enough to do some
exceptional things.

Nell
We never met a dramatist before.
Tell us what you write about.

Paul
My last play was about music.

Roger
Before he begins his questions there was something
I wanted to ask Bob about the Challenger.

Nell
Music is a good subject.

Bob
That was a grim business.
They were all my friends.
We trained together for years.

Nell
It could have been him,
it was luck, he wasn't selected for that crew.

Bob
I love music, I like to listen to Handel
when I am in orbit.

Nell
I expect you can see now
how we could be anybody.
I could be the wife of a pilot, or a cop, or a diver.

Judy
That's what I said (forgive me Bob),
why are astronauts interesting?

Roger
The shuttle wasn't destroyed was it?
I heard they dredged most of it up.

Paul
I am interested, that's enough for me.

Nell
The one about music, I'd like to see that.

Bob
The booster rocket exploded
but the shuttle was completely intact
when they took it out of the ocean.

Roger
And the people inside . . . ?

Bob
They were there.

Judy
Beats me to see why this is interesting,
when there are an endless number of people and stories
you could choose from?

Paul
I am interested in science and technology
and to me the space programme represents
the peak of technological aspiration.

Bob
He's right.

Nell
I love the theatre.

Roger
What happened to them?

Bob
They were liquefied.
The vibration and high pressure
reduced them to human jelly in their flight suits.

Roger
What a death,
and it could have been you.

Bob
That's what I thought.

Nell
I never heard this before.

Roger
Only bags of bones?

Bob
No bones left.

Judy
Do you need to know this?
We've just had dinner!

Bob
Could you put that in a play?

Paul
Anything's possible in theatre.

Nell
They wouldn't have known anything would they?
It must have been instant, wasn't it?

Bob
Not necessarily, as the temperature and pressure built up
they may have lost consciousness
but they could have taken as long as eight minutes to die.
We'll never know exactly.

Judy
Isn't there a safety procedure?

Bob
We rehearse bailing out
but we could never do it at that speed.

Roger
A one-way ticket.
When you've got a mission coming up
doesn't it frighten you?

Nell
He has one in twenty-six days.

Bob
You learn all you can
so you know the risks
and then you accept that.

Nell (*to* **Paul**)
Are you going to go to the theatre while you're here?

Paul
What should I see?

Roger
The film of *The Right Stuff* is being shown.
You should see that.

Bob
No one understands how dangerous the space shuttle is.
There are millions of things that can go wrong:

we rely on every instrument to work at its peak capacity
yet each flight reveals hundreds of new flaws!

Roger
So it could go bang at any moment of the flight?

Bob
On our last flight the outer windscreen was damaged,
hit by a flake of paint less than a millimetre in size.
The atmosphere is getting more cluttered
and the risk is growing all the time.
Pieces of space junk collide and divide in orbit
creating more and more bits of debris.

Roger
So at that speed a large piece could destroy the shuttle?

Bob
Yes.

Nell
Perhaps your play about astronauts will be done here in
Houston?

Bob
You should visit the Opera House.
We went to the première of Michael Tippett's *New Year*,
I liked it but of course they got the spacecraft all wrong.

Roger
I don't now if I could live with the possibility of sudden
death always hanging over me.

Nell
Paul hasn't asked any of his questions yet.

Paul
How can you deal with the risk that Bob lives with?

Bob
Good question.

Nell
I can't.

Judy
You needn't have answered that.

Nell
I wanted to say it.

Judy
What kind of thing are you going to write?

Paul
It'll be a piece of fiction.
(*To* **Nell**.) I promise I won't quote you or portray you.

Nell
Why have you come to talk to us then?

Paul
It's research.

Bob
Do you use a computer?

Paul
No, I write directly on paper.

Bob
Hard work?

Paul
There aren't many words in a play,
so the work's not in writing them down
but in thinking them up.

7

Alex *and* **Stone**.

Alex
Is there something else I can do now?

Stone
What else could anyone do?

Alex
No, you misunderstand; I just want a job.

Stone
This is your job now: to be what you are, for life.

Alex
What do I do?

Stone
We want to observe you
and we need to use you.
You want to further our work don't you?

Alex
How can I live like this?
Everywhere I go people smile at me.
There are no strangers any more.

Stone
Relax, all these people love you.
You belong to them now.

Alex
But have I changed?
Or has the world changed?
Is it everyone else that's changed?

Stone
You've see things no one else has seen.
They imagine you must know things no one else knows.
I shouldn't dwell on it.

Alex
You know how if you repeat a word endlessly
it becomes nonsense?
I've repeated my story so many times
it has become meaningless.

Stone
Why should you have to talk?

Alex
Why should I have to talk?

Stone
There's no need for you to speak directly to the press ever
again.
I can get a writer to write speeches for you.

Alex
Good.
If I didn't have to speak life would be easier.

Stone
You can write your autobiography now.

Alex
But I am so young.

Stone
It needn't be long.

Alex
How can I write a book about an hour in space?

Stone
Everyone wants to know about you.

Alex
What is there to tell?
My childhood was like any other.

Stone
You once said your father, when he was a child,
ran seven miles just to see an aeroplane land.

Alex
Yes, it's true.

Stone
That would be a good place to start.

Alex
Before I was born?

Stone
People will be inspired to know that you had a childhood like
any other.
Everything that ever happened to you is significant now,
in retrospect.
Think about that.

Alex
I can't write.

Stone
I'll get a writer who can write your autobiography
and your speeches.

Alex
Why did you pick me?

Stone
Why do you ask that question,

when you know the answer?
Don't you?

Alex
I'm sorry.

Stone
I understand that you are human.

8

Nell
If you could speak out
and tell people who you were
you might expect to be understood
but who would listen?

When they selected the first non-astronaut
to go into space
they chose a teacher
because teachers are trained communicators.

NASA was looking for the person
who could do the best job of describing
the experience of being on the shuttle
to the most people on earth.

Ten finalists were picked
from twelve thousand applicants
and when they announced the one
who was to fly on the Challenger,
I was at the White House:
we were guests for the day.

By chance
we were trapped in an elevator
with all ten candidates,
and I noticed the name of the manufacturer
because it was a company
who built parts of the Challenger itself.

She was standing next to me
the girl they chose;
a social historian

who had developed a course in the American Woman.
Now each of the teachers had a different project
so while we waited
for the repair men
she explained her idea.
It was simple.

It was to write a journal of the space flight,
no one had attempted that before.
'I believe history should be told in the words
of the common people,'
she said.

9

Anna *and* **Alex**.

Anna
Did you get a new job?

Alex
No but I don't have to speak any more.
A writer is going to write my speeches
and my autobiography.

Anna
People are only interested in what you did.
They forget we lived before
and have to live afterwards too.
Did you ask for more money?

Alex
No.

Anna
You are too generous with yourself.

Alex
Don't be mercenary.
We have a lot more now;
we don't want.

Anna
You forget how we lived.
You forget the ice on the inside of the window.

Alex
Don't you see there's more to this?

Anna
What other purpose could there be
than the betterment of our lives?
Isn't that what's behind it all?
Isn't that what this is about?

Alex
I don't know.
I've seen things no one else has seen,
I know things no one else knows
and somehow I have to live with it.
Can you imagine what that's like?

Anna
Yes.

Alex
Recently when I've told people,
I wonder they believe it.
It hardly seems true to me any more.

Anna
When you first came back and told me
I knew it was true then.

Alex
The words and experiences were close together.
I think the first time you say something it's real;
after that it becomes a story.

Anna
You have no reason to bear this alone.
Is there anything left you haven't told?

Alex
Only you and I will ever know?

Anna
Is this something I wouldn't expect to hear?

Alex
Light passed through my head, in space.

Anna
Did you close your eyes?
Everyone sees light when they close their eyes.

Alex
It went right in through my head!
In here, behind my forehead
there were flickers of light in here.

Anna
No wonder you didn't tell anyone.

Alex
What do you think it was?

Anna
Lightning?

Alex
That would be painful.
I felt no pain at all.

Anna
Has it affected your mind?
Have there been any after-effects?

Alex
No but perhaps they'll discover something when they dissect
my brain?

Anna
If it's brain damage you'll need treatment
before the autopsy stage.

Alex
How would you feel if I was shown to be a fake?

Anna
We'd lose everything
but as far as I am concerned you'd be the same person.

Alex
I think even if there's damage
no one could tell I was aware.
Now, even if I can't do anything else:
by not speaking
I shall exist as myself again

rather than only as what I did.
No one will know what I haven't told
and life will be more straightforward.

Anna
Until it happens again.

Alex
To me?

Anna
To others,
on other flights
in the future.
What if someone else gets light passing though their head?

Alex
What can I do?

Anna
You have to hope your experience was unique.

10

In the restaurant. As 6: **Nell**, **Bob**, **Roger**, **Paul** *and* **Judy**. **Nell**
and **Bob** *talk aside while* **Roger** *lectures* **Paul** *and* **Judy** *watches*.

Nell
What other horrors are there?

Bob
I wanted to protect you from that.

Nell
Too late, now it's time I knew everything.

Roger
Have you got an idea of the scale of the Universe?
Here's a way of thinking of it:
everyone sees the moon, you can imagine how far that is.
If this piece of paper, the thickness of it,
stands for the distance to the moon,
how tall would the stack be
to represent the distance to the sun?

Nell
This matters to you more than life itself doesn't it?

Paul *is listening to* **Nell** *and* **Bob**.

Roger (*to* **Paul**)
How tall would it be?

Bob (*to* **Nell**)
I know I am blessed you see.

Paul
Let me think about that.

Nell (*to* **Bob**)
I need to know of these dangers.

Bob
I don't know everything.

Nell
What am I being protected from?

Bob
It's me that's at risk.

Roger (*to* **Paul**)
Yes?

Nell (*to* **Bob**)
You rely on my support
yet you keep me in ignorance of your true situation?

Paul (*to* **Roger**)
Tell me.

Roger
It would be ninety miles high.

Nell (*to* **Bob**)
Am I to hide my concern from you?

Roger
Now search further in your mind
to the heart of the galaxy
within which our solar system exists.
If the thickness of this paper
stands for the distance to the moon,

how tall would the stack be
to represent the distance to the centre of the Milky Way?

Nell (*to* **Bob**)
How can you know you are blessed?

Roger (*to* **Paul**)
Well?

Paul
What?

Bob *exits to go to the Gents.*

Roger
Are you listening?

Judy
It would stretch from here to the sun.

Roger
That's the right answer.
Who told you that?

Paul
Does that make you feel insignificant?

Roger
No, not when it's me that's saying it.

Judy *takes* **Nell** *aside.*

Judy
Can you give me a lift home?

Nell
Yes, let's get out of here.

Judy
If we don't leave now
we'll become the subject of this.

Nell
Did I say too much?

Judy
How do you know he won't quote you?

Nell
I am not an astronaut am I?

Judy
You realise my husband's just 'playing up to camera'.

Nell
Was that what Bob did?

Roger
People say they can't imagine
an edge to the Universe
but when you look at the night sky
some of the light that reaches your eye
came from the edge of the Universe.
It started travelling at the beginning of time
and meets your eye tonight.

Paul
You mean the eye can see further
than the mind can stretch?

Nell
I feel sick.

Judy
I'm a doctor.

Nell
Do you think Bob wants to die?
I know I could get over it if he didn't come back.

Judy
How can you know that?

Nell
It would be easier than this.

Judy
You only think that.

Nell
He built a window in the kitchen ceiling
so that I shouldn't forget him in orbit
then I saw him falling through it in a burning space suit.

Judy
A day-dream.

Nell
How can I live with my imagination
when I discover the facts are worse?

Paul (*to* **Roger**)
I can try to imagine an edge to the Universe
but there's always going to be space beyond isn't there?

Roger
No, I know that the Universe is finite
because the night sky is dark;
if it were infinite then the sky would be bright
with the light of infinite stars
wouldn't it?

Bob *returns*.

Judy
We're leaving you to talk.

Bob
I'll come, let's all go now.

Nell
No, you can fucking stay and answer the questions.

Judy (*to* **Roger**)
You can see us to the car.

Paul
Good night.

Judy *and* **Nell** *exit with* **Roger**.

Bob
I can't stay long.

Paul
He's tactless isn't he?

Bob
I'm used to blunt questions.
At least he didn't ask how the cost can be justified
when people are starving.

Paul
What is it you do exactly?

Bob
I'm the pilot.
My job is to land the space shuttle,
the wings enable it to glide down onto a runway
but as there's no engine,
there's no chance of flying round again
so I have to get it right, first time, each time.

Paul
How can you do that?

Bob
It's skill. I am the best pilot.

Paul
In what way best?

Bob
I'm kidding you.
We have a computer.
I am a technician.

Roger *has returned.*

Roger
Why don't they land with parachutes,
like they used to,
then the shuttle wouldn't need wings?

Bob
He's right, the wings are the source of all the trouble.
They stress the whole craft and make launching
problematic as the Challenger showed.

Paul
Why does it have wings then?

Roger
They need your keys, they're waiting outside.

Bob
The shuttle needs wings so it can land after a single orbit.

Paul
Why?

Bob
This was part of the original brief from Congress . . .

Roger
Keys!

Bob
So it could drop a bomb
and land without passing over again.

Roger
Shall I drop your keys out to her?

Bob
No, I'll go, I'll take them both home.
It's no problem.

Bob *exits*.

Paul
You drove him away.
Did you need to hammer him with questions?

Roger
I want to know what it's like.

Paul
Remember I'm the one that's doing research here.

Roger
I suggested this dinner.

Paul *takes the bill*.

Paul
How shall we pay this?

Roger
You have the grant.

Paul
The more I learn the less I can imagine
who would want to be an astronaut.

Roger
I can.
If you are an astronomer
eventually you get the urge to stick your head
out into the Universe itself.
Perhaps I'll find what I'm looking for that way?

Paul
You think you have a chance?
This is something you mean to do?

Judy *re-enters but* **Roger** *does not notice.*

Roger
It's what's most important to me,
becoming an astronaut and getting into space.

Paul *sees* **Judy**.

Paul
What about your wife?
How does she fit into this?

Roger
She asks if I'd give up my work for her sake!

Judy *hits* **Roger**.

Judy
Bob's car won't start,
we all have to go now.

11

Bob
I was born in the most affluent nation on earth.
A secure home filled me with confidence.
As a young man my ambition was encouraged
but I never felt the need to be competitive.
I was always first at whatever I did.

When I applied to join the corps
they showed me ink blots.
To me they always looked the same.
Always the same part of the female anatomy.
I knew I couldn't say that each time
so I had to find other images.

A volcano. A horse's head.
A forest reflected in water. An iceberg.
A butterfly. The Milky Way.
Deep sea creatures.

Some people look and find oblivion,
patches of doubt merging to block out the light.
You can fall head first through the paper
out of yourself and into madness.

When I said,
'The shape on the paper is the shape of the Milky Way,'
the psychiatrist told me
that the ancients believed the Milky Way
was the path between Heaven and Earth.
Isn't that neat? I got the job.

And so,
speaking for myself:
because no car hit me in the street,
because the cancer did not bite,
because my parents met at all,
and I am here:

how can I not know that I am blessed?

12

Anna *and* **Alex**. **Bob** *and* **Paul**. *These two dialogues exist
independent of each other.*

Anna (*reads from a book entitled 'Look to the Sky'*)
'You must envisage the earth beneath you, very blue, more
blue than you could imagine and all the colours vivid and
bright. No photograph can show the brightness of these
colours. The earth is turning. The light of the sun illuminates
everything against the dark of space but when the earth
obscures the sun then you are in the black itself with only
stars; and the bulk of the earth shows as darkness where
there's no star.'

Alex
When I hear that I am there.

Bob
Truth ought to be more exciting than fiction
but there's been a big failure of communication.

People are more interested in sci-fi
than the reality of what we do,
that's why we had Disney build us a visitor centre here.

Paul
Thanks for agreeing to talk more.
After last night I wondered if you'd care to see me again.

Bob
We need people to understand what we do now,
that's why we're all keen to do what we can to help you.

Paul
Can I go to a launch?

Bob
Sure, we'll get a schedule and you can pick a flight.

Paul
I'll come to yours.

Bob
OK.

Anna
Are these your words?
Have you even read your autobiography?

Alex
I wasn't interested in what he wrote
but I'll read it if there's more like that.

Anna
What does it say about me in here?
I didn't meet this writer.
What does he know about me?

Bob
Would you like to go into space yourself?

Paul
Me, frankly I'd rather burn in hell;
but on the other hand, if I got the chance to go I'd go.

Bob
They've always wanted to send a writer

or an artist of some kind,
someone who could communicate the experience through art.

Paul
That's what I am doing here.

Bob
We thought a musician or a composer would be best and
they proposed the singer John Denver
but then the whole idea was abandoned after Challenger.

Alex
What does it matter if the whole thing is invented?
Let people believe what they choose.

Anna
It means I don't exist.

Alex
You exist.
You live and breathe and have thoughts don't you?
I'm telling you you exist.

Anna
Yes but not in there.

Paul
When it's so dangerous why are people
still going into space?

Bob
Listen, some people will tell you there's a one-in-six chance
of the shuttle exploding each time it flies
but if it had to be entirely safe
no one could ever go into space
(or walk down the street for that matter).
No one is asked to be an astronaut but plenty want to do it.

Anna (*reads again*)
'I shared with her my dream of flight.'
It was me who dreamed of flight.

Alex
Some dream of yours?
Most people don't even recall their dreams.

Anna
Did you tell him?

Alex
He did research.

Anna
Where does this all come from?

Alex
His imagination, where else?

Paul
Let me ask you something.
When you first went into space
what surprised you?

Bob
Nothing. There were no surprises.

Paul
Nothing? What about the flaws in the shuttle itself?

Bob
(Usually those are only discovered afterwards.)
No, we have very good training,
we simulate each mission many times:
we want to minimise the challenge to an astronaut.

Anna
So this is fiction!

Alex
Neither of us exists then: I am not in it either.

Anna
It's your autobiography! It says what you did.

Alex
He consulted the technicians

to write an account of operating the craft
when I didn't do anything.

Paul
You insulate yourself against the experience?

Bob
We aim to eliminate the unknown.
In each simulation we test the crew
with some unexpected event
and they have to deal with it,
so that when it comes to going into space for real
it's a relief there are no surprises.
Sometimes people say it's less exciting than the simulation.

Anna
Everyone knows what you did.

Alex
What I did?
I saw. I ate. I took pictures.
Apart from that it happened to me.
I was simply there.
I sat there.
I could only look.

Anna
You had controls.

Alex
Automatic. I couldn't touch them.
Only in an emergency would they have given me the code to
unlock them.

Paul
So tell me about this failure of communication?

Bob
Congress needs a reason to let us do this,
once it was military expediency:
we demonstrated our superior technology to the world

but the end of the Cold War was a great loss,
now the Space Race is finished
and the thing itself isn't enough of a reason.

Anna
No one knows that you didn't do anything.

Alex
What am I if I didn't do anything:
the pilot or the passenger?
Perhaps it could have been anyone?

Anna
It couldn't have been me.

Alex
What shall I do?
If there's not this then there isn't anything.

Anna
You're alive.

Alex
So?

Anna
You're not allowed to complain.
You were the first man in space.

Bob
What's happened: I see it like the discovery of fire
or the invention of language.

People's indifference puzzles me.

What went wrong?
Has the media failed us?
Or is it that no one believed it from the start?

I always thought everyone wants to think
they live at a significant time; and we do.
This is where there's been a failure,
no one understands it for itself.

Paul
You know, you've been an astronaut.
How can someone else?

Bob
I'm hoping your play will help us with that.
And now that I'm inviting you to a launch
I'm also hoping you'll ignore what my wife said last night.

Anna
What is the value of all this
if no one is to know what it's really like?

Alex
Perhaps you're asking for the impossible?

Anna
But I know.

Alex
Or do you *think* you know?

Anna
What do *you* know?

Alex
You forget, the object was simply to send a man
and bring him back safely.
I've done all that is required of me.
I just have to remain healthy,
pulse normal, breathing regular:
show how unaffected I am by this experience.

Anna
Unless you are affected you could be a stand-in for yourself.

Paul
Are you telling me it's all over,
the manned exploration of space?

Bob
Where is there to go?
There's plenty of space out there
but it's all too far away.

Paul
You've been lucky then?

Bob
Two flights in the last ten years
and another coming up.
I am one of the favoured few.

Alex
I've done my best.
I am not a poet or a philosopher.
The achievement consists in the act not in the telling.

Anna
You owe it to us all.

Alex
What do I owe?
I've told all I could tell.

Anna
Aren't you forgetting something?

Alex
I'm sure I've forgotten most of it now
apart from what I could never put into words,
and no one can take that from me.
I must have something to hold on to.
The experience was mine alone,
I risked my life for it.
My vision.

Anna
Your vision?
My dream.

Paul
And what did you learn?

Bob
I saw the change:
the planet has turned from blue to grey in ten years.

Paul
That must have been a surprise?

Bob
Yes.

13

Alex, **Dan** *and* **Carl**.

Alex
No?

Dan
That day I was glad not to be chosen.

Carl
None of us wanted to be chosen but you.

Alex
We competed like dogs!

Dan
I was happy to be the standby.

Alex
So you both lied.

Carl
None of us could have admitted this then.

Alex
Why are you telling me?

Dan
We felt a duty to square with you now.

Alex
Don't you trust the machinery?

Carl
No, I know you can trust a machine
in a way you can never trust a person.

Dan
It's easy to have faith now
but it seemed remote then.

I was sick when they launched the rocket.
Between us here, I don't know if I could have kept my mind.

Alex
Have no fear of madness,
it's just a question of keeping a sense of proportion.
I had no disturbance.
My mind was clear the whole time.
You don't change.
Everything is the same.
It's simply that everyone thinks you've changed.

Carl
Thanks to you,
I am happy to be next, we both are.

Alex
What if you had been chosen first?

Carl
It's clear now that you were the only possible choice then.
None of us understood the source of your courage.
The way you spoke that day, it was philosophical.
We didn't recognise what we heard.

Alex
What did I say?

Dan
I've read your book over and over;
the bit about your childhood,
it was just like mine.

Alex
Weren't all our childhoods the same?

Carl
And yet we are different people.

Dan
I've already imagined myself in space,
reading that.

Alex
No you haven't.

Dan
No, why?

Alex
Because it is more incredible than you could imagine.

Dan
Then, when I am there for real I shall see it with your eyes.

Carl
Surely the best part must be being able to tell the story
afterwards?

Dan
If I had done what you did I could die happy.
You need do nothing more, need you?

Alex
You must realise I didn't write that book?
I don't even know how I was chosen.
And I never understood why he said he wasn't being
generous.

Carl
That was in case you never came back.

Alex
It was a complete unknown.
In those hours before the flight
I was at peace with myself,
weren't we all prepared to die?

Carl
Perhaps you know how to die
but I don't want to sacrifice my life.

Alex
Scared?

Dan
It's only the moment of death that I dread.

Carl
I may not fear it but I don't invite it either;
for the sake of those I love,
I think of what my absence would subject them to.

Dan
If you died up there
you would orbit the earth for ever.

Alex
That would be immortality.

Carl
How did you say goodbye to your wife?

Enter **Stone**.

Alex
Quickly.

Stone
The day we met and I chose the first of you,
what was possible became actual then through his belief;
he staked his life on it.
Now this isn't just a possibility any more.
Here are copies of the photo we took that day.
Take them back to your families.
Let them see the courage and confidence in those faces.

That day, it was inevitable that some would be disappointed
but I kept my word and now you two are next.

Alex
I've told them all there is to know.

Stone
I can see you've no fear.

Carl
It's natural to feel concern where there's risk
but I know luck is on our side.

Dan
I feel only anticipation.
I mean to look so carefully, take in all I can.

Alex
But remember you are not paid to look.

Stone
Are you prepared to stake your lives?

Carl
We have his example.
We're ready.

Dan
Yes. I know what's going to happen.
We have a job to do.

Stone
Good.
The word from above has always been
that this can continue as long as I can guarantee success;
this man achieved 100 per cent success,
what he said was always exactly what we wanted to hear.

Alex
When my father was a child
he ran seven miles just to see an aeroplane land.

Stone
Often I think of the future that we shall never see. I could
easily go mad when I try to imagine what will happen that I
shall not know but then I think we were the first and in that
far distant future they will look back and wonder what it was
like for us in the beginning which is something they'll never
know. Then I remember what good fortune I have to be here
now.

Alex
Your genius remains a mystery to us all.

Stone
There's no mystery to a single-track mind.
Once upon a time
I shot field-mice into the air
attached to sky rockets,
they lived and I never looked back.

Dan
Can I ask a question?
(*To* **Alex**.) Your autobiography *Look to the Sky*.
Did you call it that?

Stone
It was what he said that day:

'Everyone looks to the sky.'
Why did you say it?

Alex
I was just trying the words out.

Stone
We have thirty-six hours now,
you must first go and say goodbye to your families.

14

Oliver, **Gina** *and* **Paul**. **Gina** *and* **Paul** *are looking at the moon.*

Oliver (*aside*)
I am not Neil.
It could have been me
but it wasn't.
I was disappointed then
now I get fifty letters a day,
still.
I was not the first there
but I saw what he saw
I did what he did.

I saw the rockets blow up too,
I was one of that original group
but I didn't get to fly
until years later.

No doubt you've heard stories
about the men who walked on the moon.
People will tell you we're all crazy now
but then
I took that famous photograph
of the whole earth from space
and someone even claimed it as evidence
that the earth was indeed flat.

Gina (*aside to* **Paul**)
I persuaded him to meet you
and you should know that you are honoured
because he rarely talks about it.

Paul
Well thanks, I'm down here for the launch
so this works out well for me.

Gina
It's a pleasure,
it's an excuse for me to get him talking.

On a clear night we often come out here
and watch the moon as an alternative to television.

Paul
Tonight it looks as if you could reach out and touch it.

Gina
I've touched it, with these fingers;
a piece of the moon is available for all
at the Air and Space Museum in Washington.

Paul
What is it like, is it just a rock?

Gina
No, it's beautiful,
the caress of a million fingers
has smoothed it to the consistency of polished steel.

Oliver *joins them.*

Oliver (*to* **Paul**)
You spoke to Alan Bean?

Paul
Yes.

Oliver
Nobody hassles Alan.

Paul
So I found.

Oliver
Did you call Neil?

Paul
No. I was told it would be a waste of time.

Oliver
He's not eloquent.

Paul
Tell me about being on the moon.

Oliver
When I was there I could stretch out my thumb
and cover up the earth.

Paul
That small?

Oliver
From a quarter of a million miles away
our fragile earth is the only coloured thing,
the moon is grey or biscuit brown
and space is black.
I'll show you where I was.
Do you see the areas of light on the surface?

Paul
Yes.

Oliver
The lower one to the left,
it's called the Sea of Clouds
(a wilderness without a footprint),
that's it,
that's where I was,
that's where I walked on the moon.
Can you see it?

Paul
Yes.

Oliver
I can't.

Paul
No.

Oliver
It's just a blur to me now.
It was a long time ago,
my eyesight isn't what it was
and I left my glasses inside.

Paul
I remember clearly

watching it on television
when I was a child.

Oliver
There are two places in my mind:
one is the close-up moon where I was
and this out-of-focus one up in the sky is another.

Gina
People look at the moon
and they see a light in the sky.
I had to look and tell myself: it has no light,
it does not wax and wane,
what I see is what's lit by the sun.

Oliver
She sees only what she believes.

Gina
If you believed what you saw
you'd think the moon gave its own light.

Paul (*to* **Oliver**)
And if you believed what you saw
you might think there was a blur in the sky?

Oliver
Yes, isn't it the way we perceive things
that makes them what they are?

15

Carl
I fear weakness
so I did not question.
I mistook anger for cowardice
when I am no coward:
I let anger take my voice away.

I got this chance
and took it
though I do not trust it.
I am a gambler
because I am lucky

and I got the chance
that's why I took it:
it was a gift.

Looks at the photo.

What kind of chance do I have?
Who will remember me?
Shall I get to tell the story afterwards?
I am one of the other people in this photograph.
I mistook anger for cowardice
when I am no coward,
I let anger take my voice away:
I said goodbye to my wife quickly.

What did we want?
What shall I find?
Expectation is all I have left.
It's not weakness that I fear,
I've learnt I am no coward.

16

Judy *and* **Nell**.

Judy
Speak your mind.

Nell
Part of me wants to kick,
part of me wants to yell,
part of me wants to kill.

Judy
I understand that.
I would be the same.

Nell
When we married I said to him
'I'm going to put you first in my life,
will you put me first in yours?'
Big mistake.
He expects my support and encouragement

while he intends to fly as many times as he can.
That's what he lives for really.

Judy
What about your needs?

Nell
Forget it. I do everything myself.
I mow the lawn, take out the garbage,
keep the home and family in order.
That's my contribution to the US effort in space.

Judy
This is no good for you.

Nell
It takes the skin off me like sandpaper.
At the Cape
I'll watch the NASA channel,
the kids will visit Seaworld
and for what anybody knows
we may never see him again.

Judy
You must confront him.
This demeans you.

Nell
Even the pay's no good,
he doesn't get much more than a standard pilot's wage,
I have to work.
When he doesn't fly the shuttle any more
the rewards are plenty and waiting.
Any number of companies want to have an astronaut's name
on the notepaper.
There are professorships too, even admin jobs.
(They pay the managers a lot more than the astronauts.)

Judy
You can't wait for that.
It may never happen.

Nell
I've accepted he may die.

Judy
What then?

Nell
That night,
the night we had dinner
I did confront him then.

Judy
Did he tell you he did it for you?

Nell
No, and he didn't say he couldn't do it without me.

Judy
So?

Nell
I don't hate him.

Judy
I don't understand how anyone could tolerate this.

Nell
I went out onto the lawn
and stood in the sprinkler to cool off!
I watched our family each in their separate rooms
then I lay down in the wet
and looked up into the dark.

Judy
I don't understand you.

Nell
I have no self-pity.
I know;
because of all I imagine,
even after what I've learnt;
that in his situation,
if I was him,
if I were to get the opportunity
I would take it:
I would do the same.
Wouldn't you?

Wouldn't anyone?
Wouldn't you?

Judy *does not answer but takes* **Nell** *in her arms.*

17

Stone *and* **Alex**.

Stone (*aside*)
If you have a strong idea
then you don't listen to others
because you can't afford that time
and there will always be those who disagree.

That's why I am so organised
because I don't mean to waste any time:
I work every second of the day.

You only have so many years
and I intend to use all my time
because I need to know that I lived.

Alex
You worked your whole life for this.
Why did you give it away?

Stone
I've got you.

Alex
Why not go yourself?
Why choose someone else?

Stone
The importance of an enterprise of this kind
cannot rest in any individual alone
so even if it were practical
it couldn't be me.
I knew I should never be the one.

Alex
How do I deserve this?
Why me?
I need to hear you say it.

Stone
I wanted someone with aspiration
but without doubts.

Alex
Out of all of us, only me then.
How did you tell?

Stone
What?
Why are you staring?
Have you got doubts now?

Alex
Why am I unable to do anything else?

Stone
Is something wrong?
You're well are you?
Perhaps you need a check-up.
Not drinking too much?

Alex
I've still got hopes that's all.

Stone
In life we learn to accept.
No one avoids getting old.
Ambition is something:
you could get more money;
I can give you more authority
but you refuse.
Why not find some concrete ambitions for yourself?
Abandon hope in the abstract.

Alex
I am allowed hopes.

Stone
Don't be sentimental.
Do you think I could have done what I've done through
hope.

Alex
I need hope.

Stone
I know you want to go back.
I can't imagine how it can be
to see that only once.

Alex
That's not it.

Stone
There might be a virtue in sending you again
to prove a man can do it.
But I can't take that risk.
I can't risk you now.

Alex
You talk of 100 per cent success.
You can never guarantee it will work!
This is Russian roulette:
you pull the trigger once
and it doesn't go off
so you pull the trigger again.

Stone
You're not talking rationally now.
You don't know who you are.
Ambition is something,
hopes can destroy a man.

Stone *exits*.

Alex
Being alone in space,
more alone than anyone's ever been;
I was entirely myself,
I knew where I was
and why I was there.

I looked out
and thought:
life evolved on earth,
creatures emerged from the slime
and eventually
there's me here.

In the deep silence
I heard my body working,

my heart beating,
the blood pulsing.

Then I saw my face
reflected in the glass
and noticed my teeth
how savage they look;
I've got teeth like an animal.
They're my least human bit.

Three billion people on earth.

Teeth are for biting.
My body is pulsing with hot blood
and my head is full of darkness.

18

As 14: **Paul**, **Oliver**, **Gina**.

Paul (*to* **Oliver**)
What happened to you exactly?
Is there a word for it?

Oliver
It was wonder.

Paul
Wonder?

Oliver
I was changed by it. Afterwards
I had to piece together a new world for myself,
everything had been taken away from me.

Gina
There he was trying to solve the riddle of existence
and not a penny to his name.

Paul
Surely, as an astronaut, the bank gave you credit?

Oliver
They kept my cheques for the signatures
when I first came back from the moon.

Gina
He had to make his own money to live.

Oliver
I had no money.

Gina
People think he made a lot of money
out of going to the moon.
What do you think he got?
Guess.

Paul
Tell me.

Oliver
It cost them six times my weight in gold to put me there.

Gina
What he got was thirty dollars,
in travel expenses: the moon and back.
Can you beat it?
No one could live on that.
He had to find his own living.

Paul
When you came back from the moon
how do you decide how to spend the rest of your life?

Oliver
I had to find a way to live.

Paul
Surely you could have got a job?

Gina
He was in no state to do a job at that time.

Oliver
I was shaken up.
It was an exceptional situation:
I knew I still had many years of my life in front of me.
I had to work out how to spend them.
I had to earn a living.
So I asked myself how I liked to spend time.

But where do you start?
What was I going to do?
You are wasting your time unless you can find something.
I could have done anything.
My first marriage ended then
but I wasn't going to lay down and die,
I told myself:
'You have nothing to lose.'
That's how it was when I came back from the moon.

Paul
You're not telling me what you're telling me.

Oliver
Are you a goal-orientated person?

Paul
I'm writing this play.

Oliver
I was a goal-orientated person
but I fulfilled my aspiration in one shot.
It was a morbid kind of freedom.
When you have been changed you can never go back
though life can get you down
but I know I have had my moment of ecstasy.

Gina
When we first met,
we were introduced and we shook hands.
'Hey,' I thought,
'I just touched a man who walked on the moon.'
What a feeling!
I was so aware of it
my hand seemed to swell to fill the whole room.
Then we married
and I got to touch him all over.

Paul
What's it like being married to a man who walked on the
moon?

Gina
I don't compete with him

but I am not in his shadow either.
When we got your letter
I wanted to meet you
because I've worked in the theatre too,
I am an actor.
When people see me
they hear only the lines I speak
and see only the role I play
but it isn't me. Not who I am.
That's how we came to understand each other.
Our situations are parallel.
People know him for what he did
but it isn't who he is.

Paul (*to* **Oliver**)
Who are you?

Oliver
Excuse me?
What is the question?

Paul
Did you find how to live?
You've obviously got a life here.

Oliver
I found a way to live.
I realised that what I suffered wasn't unique,
and that I could help others in similar situations.
So I set up an organisation to do it.
In fact so many Americans have a problem making contact
with reality
that we're the fastest-growing institute here in the States
now.

Gina (*to* **Paul**)
When you've done the research,
who's going to write your script?

Paul
Who? Me.

Gina
Haven't you got a ghost?

Paul
No? I'll write it.

Oliver
We know a lot of people who've done books
but I never met anyone who actually wrote one before.

Paul
So this is a first for both of us?

They shake hands. **Paul** *looks at his hand and then up at the moon.*

Gina (*aside*)
And I thought
what did he learn from that?
Did you see what got across?

Paul *exits.*

Who was he?
We never heard from him again;
perhaps it was a hoax?

Everyone wants to feel touched by it.

Fifteen years
since I married the man in the moon.
A lot changes.
For a start
every particle of your body is replaced
each seven years.
Neither of us is who we were
in any sense.

Our youngest child,
what do you think she asks me
all the time?
'What shall I do next?'

There's the pool
we jump in and out of it
all day.

This is an incredible place
where we live here
you cut the grass
and it just grows right up again.

19

Stone *and* **Anna**.

Stone
I need your help.
There's a problem.
I don't know if we can get them back alive.

Anna
Can't you do anything?

Stone
Nothing can be done until there's contact.
If we can establish a signal,
if any kind of communication is possible
an alarm bell will ring in here.
Until that happens I can only wait.
Your husband has gone to inform the families.
Logically, I know you must have some understanding
of what they may suffer.
We don't know what will happen
but they need to remain positive.
In the meantime
I'm keen they shouldn't talk to anyone else.
I need your help.
Will you go to them and stay with them?

Anna
I'll do all I can for them.

Stone
I'm grateful to you.
You'll see your husband there.
(I've got a car coming to pick you up in a few minutes.)

Anna
Before I go
in this moment now
I've got something to ask,
there's something I want to know,
about him.

Stone
What?

Anna
In confidence?

Stone
Yes.

Anna
Why did you choose him?

Stone
He is the best pilot.

Anna
I know the controls were automatic.

Stone
In an emergency
we'd have given him the code to unlock them.

Anna
A pilot with no function.

Stone
He's a brave man.

Anna
I'm proud of him.

Stone
He's modest about what he did.

Anna
It could have been an ape.

Stone
No, he is a man
he has the mind of a man,
we wanted to send him
and return him safely.

Anna
To see if he could stand it?

Stone
He carried it off so well
that I've begun to believe
that perhaps any adult
could be capable of this.

Anna
Anyone at all?

Stone
If they were healthy,
even a woman: though women's minds are weaker
and the bodies stranger.

Anna
I've no doubt you could find a strong woman
with a mind of her own.

Stone
It was a difficult choice we had the first time.
We had to choose someone
if it hadn't been him it would have been another.

Anna
But you did choose.
How did you choose?

Stone
We wanted a representative response.

Anna
Is representative like average?

Stone
None of them had an unusual intelligence or imagination.
He was average.

Anna
He thinks he is the best pilot.

Stone
They were all top pilots in different ways.
We didn't want to choose anyone who was exceptional within
the confines of the group.
He was the least distinctive.

Anna
Ordinary.

Stone
Yes, shouldn't that be enough for anyone?
Doesn't it reflect well on him

that an ordinary man did this?
There's no shame in it is there?

Anna
I won't tell him.

Stone
Why do you need to know this?
Have there been after-effects?
Is he holding anything to himself?

Anna
No.

Stone
Is there a domestic problem?
Has he changed?

Anna
No. He says I treat him differently now,
but then, I learnt he was prepared to say goodbye to me
for the sake of this.

Stone
You resent it?

Anna
No. I discovered that I exist independent of him.

Stone
These are harsh words.

Anna
When I met him, he was already a pilot,
I had never been in a plane.

Stone
Are you jealous?

Anna
No. I wouldn't choose this.

Stone
You prefer the domestic world?

Anna
We had aspirations and dreams
but we were small-minded

(I asked him if he had seen God),
and we were poor.
I never knew there were so many countries in the world until
we visited them all.

Stone
Why doesn't the car come?
I need you to go now.

Anna
How do you manage to look innocent
when you are so guilty?

Stone
Responsible
but not guilty.
People have died when bridges collapse
but bridges are still built.

Anna
What will happen to these men?
How will they die?

Stone
If we didn't continue
then the sacrifices of thousands of engineers
who worked for this would be in vain.
At the end of the war they would have closed this place down
but I said I could create something here,
if I have achieved anything
it is that I took the missiles I designed then
and turned them to a peaceful use now.

Anna
But why? Why?
Tell me why.

Stone
Have you any idea of the pain this causes me?

Alex *has entered,* **Stone** *sees him.*

Stone
I told you you had no reason to be grateful

and you have no reason to be ungrateful either.
I was neither generous nor ungenerous to you.
You chose to put yourself forward and you were chosen.

Alex
I wish I was an exceptional person
or had something unique to say.

Stone
What did you expect: transformation?
(*Aside.*) Why?
What is this question?
Why?
What does it mean?
WHY?

Alarm bell rings.

20

Paul *and* **Sylvie**.

Paul (*reads from a book*)
'Eight years after his epoch-making first spaceflight Gagarin
was killed when the plane he was piloting crashed on a
routine flight. Rumour and conjecture have gathered around
this event. If it was suicide no one can ascribe a motive,
equally no one can explain how such an *exceptional* pilot could
make such a tragic error.'

Sylvie
How is that relevant?

Paul
The American experience cannot be the whole story.

Sylvie
Isn't this about us,
what you're doing?

Paul
How could I write about you?
What do I know about you?

Sylvie
Why the fuck are you here then?
What have you learnt?

Paul
I've no conclusion
but my hands are dirty now,
I'm culpable.

Sylvie
You can't evade having an opinion.

Paul
I'll choose what I write
just as you can choose what you tell me.
I wanted to speak to some astronauts here,
and cosmonauts in Russia,
find out what the experience was in common, OK?

Sylvie
I've been thinking about your question
'What is it like in space?'

Paul
Yes.

Sylvie
There are several questions there.

You are asking how does it feel,
what is the experience of being there?
What *is* it like?

You are asking what kind of environment
what kind of place is it?
What is *it* like?

You are asking to compare the experience
with another experience.
What *is* it 'like'?

You are asking to compare the environment
with another environment.
What is *it* 'like'?

My answer was the answer only to the first question.
'What *is* it like?'

Paul
'More incredible than you could imagine.'
Give me some other answers.
What is *it* like?

Sylvie
Space is empty.
Empty space.

Paul
What *is* it 'like?'

Sylvie
What is *it* 'like?'
These questions have the same answer.
It is unlike anything.
There is an absence of all that's familiar.

Paul
I was told the training was designed to eliminate the unknown.
Someone told me there were no surprises.
'More incredible than you could imagine'?
By that token every experience is a surprise.
It doesn't mean anything does it?
It's bullshit.

Sylvie
Yeah. You can say that
but when everything is full of wonder
why should we let it become mundane?

For fifteen years the astronauts colluded
to conceal the existence of flicker flashes,
the micro-meteorites that pass through the brain in space.

They are small enough to enter and exit through the walls of
the craft and we only know they exist because they create a
sensation of light when they pass through the retina.

This was experienced from the start
but no one dared admit it because it seemed too strange.

Paul
Why did you say you had no imagination?

Sylvie
Because we need to deal only in reality
when our lives are on the line.
When that rocket goes today
a charge equivalent to the entire national grid
will be in one place at one moment.

Paul
Why did you choose to become an astronaut?
Tell me honestly.
There must be a personal reason.

Sylvie
Perhaps it was
because I always dreamed of flight?
As I'm sure you're aware
it is one of the most common female fantasies.

Paul
How would I know that?

Sylvie
We're of an age (I imagine)
I was born in '61
the first year of spaceflight;
for me, this is what happened in our lives.
I wanted to be at the centre of it.
That's why I am here.

Paul
And you still feel you are ordinary?

Sylvie
The population of the earth is over five billion now,
who cannot feel that?

Paul
Do you think I've been wasting your time?

Sylvie
I am one of the standby crew today.
I've nothing else to do.
It was my decision.
I did choose to speak to you.

Paul
I am an interloper.
Why should you trust me?

Sylvie
When I see your play
then I'll find out the truth.

21

Paul
No one dares expect what will happen
when they see a rocket go.

At ignition there's light
many times stronger than the sun.
Nothing prepares you for it,
no one warns you.
The image stays on the eye.

You expect a sound.
There is no sound
until it hits you like a kick in the chest
and the air splits apart
with the force of cast iron breaking.

The shuttle barely moves.

Slowly it leaves the earth.

Paul *begins to rise into the air.*

You pray it will work.

You watch until there's just the light
and then
in a moment
that's gone too.

You realise: it went through the roof of the sky.

Then
you look again
and you see
only a trace

of white smoke
in the form
of
a
question mark,
hanging in the air.

Paul *plunges upwards into the blue, tearing the sky as if it were*
paper and vanishing from sight. The sky falls away and the Universe
is revealed in which the earth spins revealed only by points of light on
the surface. Then the light of the sun illuminates the whole planet and
passes over, giving a sequence of night to day and back to night.

Methuen Drama Modern Plays

include work by

Jean Anouilh
John Arden
Margaretta D'Arcy
Peter Barnes
Brendan Behan
Edward Bond
Bertolt Brecht
Howard Brenton
Simon Burke
Jim Cartwright
Caryl Churchill
Noël Coward
Sarah Daniels
Nick Dear
Shelagh Delaney
David Edgar
Dario Fo
Michael Frayn
Paul Godfrey
John Guare
Peter Handke
Declan Hughes
Terry Johnson
Kaufman & Hart
Barrie Keeffe

Larry Kramer
Stephen Lowe
Doug Lucie
John McGrath
David Mamet
Arthur Miller
Mtwa, Ngema & Simon
Tom Murphy
Peter Nichols
Joe Orton
Louise Page
Luigi Pirandello
Stephen Poliakoff
Franca Rame
Philip Ridley
David Rudkin
Willy Russell
Jean-Paul Sartre
Sam Shepard
Wole Soyinka
C. P. Taylor
Theatre Workshop
Sue Townsend
Timberlake Wertenbaker
Victoria Wood